VIRGINIA ELY is widely recognized as religious writer and anthologist, appearing frequently as speaker before church, school and social organizations. A medical librarian at the United States Public Health Service Hospital in Fort Worth, Texas, she was previously engaged in denominational work with the Southern Baptist Convention. Miss Ely is the author of nine books.

DEDICATION SERVICES FOR ALL OCCASIONS

VIRGINIA ELY

《 》

Fleming H. Revell Company

WESTWOOD, NEW JERSEY

ACKNOWLEDGMENTS

I wish to acknowledge my debt of gratitude to the individuals and institutions listed below who have generously granted me permission to use materials quoted in this book.

A diligent effort has been made to identify authorship and ownership, and to give proper credit for the use of all copyrighted materials. If there has been any infringement on the rights of any author or publisher, a satisfactory adjustment will be made with the owner, and proper credit will be given in future editions.

Adams, Faye Carr, for "That Book is Good" and "Rejoice and Sing."

Broadman Press, for "God Give Us Christian Homes," by B. B. McKinney; "A Teacher Prays," by Marjorie McMahan; "The Measure," by Clarence Edwin Flynn.

Crowell, Grace Noll, for "The Quiet Hour."

Flynn, Clarence Edwin, for "Compensation."

Harper & Row, Publishers, for the following materials found in *Masterpieces of Religious Verse*: "Above the Hills of Time," by Thomas Tiplady; "Almighty Lord, With One Accord," by Melancton Woolsey Stryker; "Begin the Day With God," author unknown; "Dedication," by Louise F. Benson; "Goshen," by Edgar Frank; "O Young and Fearless Prophet," by S. Ralph Harlow.

Moody Press, for "Hidden Springs," by R. L. Constable; "A Mother's Prayer," by Barbara Ryberg.

Morrill, Belle Chapman, for "The Cloak of Love."

Peck, Kathryn Blackburn, for "Lead Wisely, Father."

Saltenstall, William, for "Where Do You Stand?"

Signs of the Times, for "When Children Pray," by Hazel Hartwell Simon.

The Scripture quotations so identified are from the *Revised Standard Version of the Bible*, copyrighted 1946 and 1952.

Contents

DEDICATION SERVICE FOR:

A Church Building (No. 1)	5
A Church Building (No. 2)	9
A Religious Education Building	11
A Christian Flag	15
The National Flag	16
The Home	19
A Home in Which There Are Young Children	21
A New Home	26
A Home for Convalescents	28
A Hospital	31
A Church Library	36
A Public Library	38
A School Library	41
Table Service for the Lord's Supper	44
A Mission Building	47
An Organ	51
A Prayer Chapel	54
A Public School Building	56
Trees	59
A Youth Center	61

To my nieces and nephews—
Freda, Frances Ann, Patti,
Bob, and Ron

A Church Building (No. 1)

MEDITATIONS IN MELODY: "Holy, Holy, Holy" (Reginald Heber, John B. Dykes), instrumental music.

CALL TO WORSHIP (read by pastor and congregation): "Come, bless the Lord, all you servants of the Lord, who stand by night in the house of the Lord! Lift up your hands to the holy place, and bless the Lord!" (PSALM 134, RSV).

MUSIC: "O Worship the King" (Robert Grant, Franz Joseph Haydn), by choir and congregation.

SCRIPTURE READING: PSALM 84, RSV, read responsively by pastor and people.

PASTORAL PRAYER

MUSIC: "Glorious Things of Thee Are Spoken" (John Newton, Franz Joseph Haydn), by choir. (If preferred, the hymn poem may be read.)

DEVOTIONAL MESSAGE: In Paul's Letter to the Ephesians we read: ". . . Christ also loved the church, and gave himself for it; That he might sanctify . . . to himself a glorious church, not having spot, or wrinkle, or any such thing; but that it should be holy and without blemish" (EPHESIANS 5:25B-27).

Because of its divine nature, three glories belong to the church which do not belong to any earthly institution:

The church has the glory of divine origin. God Almighty established only two institutions on earth: the home, which had its beginning in the Garden of Eden; and the church, which Christ our Lord formed and fashioned according to His own will even before He was offered for our redemption. Solomon's temple, which is a type of the church, was made of prepared material— drawn out, set apart for sacred service. The church also is composed of prepared material—redeemed people who have been cleansed from sin by the atoning blood of Christ, transformed into new creatures through the glorious grace of God, and called into sacred service by the Holy Spirit.

Before He ascended back to the Father, our Lord had placed

in the keeping of the young church everything it was supposed to have in order to fulfill its mission on earth—except one thing: it had the full gospel; it had the ordinances (baptism and the Lord's Supper); and it had its commission to go, teach, preach, and baptize, with further instructions to wait in Jerusalem until the coming of the Holy Spirit. That promise was fulfilled on the day of Pentecost when, after Peter had stood up and talked, proving by the Scriptures that Jesus of Nazareth was the fulfillment of all prophecy concerning the coming of the Anointed One, ". . . there were added unto them about three thousand souls" (ACTS 2:41). "And the Lord added to the church daily such as should be saved" (ACTS 2:47). The church was in existence before Pentecost, and those who were saved during those Spirit-filled days were added to it. If it had been organized on the day of Pentecost, the church would have been an organization originating in the minds of men. The church is more than an organization; it is an organism originating in the mind of God and deriving its life from the loving heart of God. One of the glories of the church which sets it apart from earthly organizations is its divine origin.

The church has the glory of divine infilling. "Ye must be born again," said Jesus to Nicodemus (JOHN 3:7). Under the guidance of the Holy Spirit, the Apostle Paul was moved to say, ". . . if any man be in Christ, he is a new creature . . ." (II CORINTHIANS 5:17). Paul refuted by his own testimony, born out of his own experience, one of the most common heresies of today—that it makes no difference what a man believes if he is sincere in his belief. Saul the Pharisee was ardently sincere in his belief when he zealously devoted himself to the persecution of Christians. One day, however, as he watched a Christian die, conviction struck at the heart of the religious zealot. Doubtless he tried to close the door of his heart to the pleadings of the Spirit; but as he journeyed toward Damascus with the avowed purpose of seizing others who were witnesses to the Way, he heard the voice of the Risen Christ calling him by name; and through the transforming grace of God, Saul the persecutor became Paul the preacher. Not only did he become known by a new name, but he had a new nature. Thereafter, when the way became rough for the bondservant of Christ, he refreshed his faith by recalling his conversional experience. He used it in his defense before Agrippa. He never grew weary with telling it. The change that was wrought in Paul on the Damascus Road moved him to say, ". . . I live; yet not I, but Christ liveth in me . . ." (GALATIANS 2:20). An unregenerated person cannot make such a statement.

"As many as believed were baptized," we often read in the New Testament. Their belief was more than mere intellectual assent to the truths that were taught; it was a belief based on repentance, a godly sorrow for sin, and a faith unto salvation. One of the glories of the church which sets it apart from earthly institutions is that it is filled with twice-born, transformed individuals.

The church has the glory of divine protection. Certainly the Lord's blessing has been upon the efforts and activities of many earthly organizations and institutions. We believe devoutly that God's hand was upon the hands of the founding fathers of our honored nation as they affixed their signatures to the Declaration of Independence; but to no nation has He said, ". . . lo, I am with you alway" (MATTHEW 28:20). No sooner had the Saviour ascended to the Father than Satan launched vicious attacks against the new church and new Christians. All through the ages he has worked with frenzied, frantic, fanatic zeal in his efforts to stop short the spread of the gospel by suppressing the reading of the Word, forbidding the assembly of believers, and inflicting the most torturous persecutions upon those who dared to bear the cross for our Lord. But the promise which Jesus made concerning His church has not failed: ". . . the gates of hell shall not prevail against it" (MATTHEW 16:18). One of the glories of the church which sets it apart from earthly institutions is its divine protection.

MUSIC: "I Love Thy Kingdom, Lord" (Timothy Dwight, Aaron Williams), choir and congregation.

Pastor: Who presents this building for dedication?

People: We, the members of this church.

Pastor: To the glory of God the Father who saves us and keeps us by his marvelous grace;

To the blessing, and glory, and honor, and power of God the Son who loved us so much that He gave Himself for us, and who ever lives to make intercession for us;

To the praise of God the Holy Spirit who calls us, directs us, and teaches us even how to pray:

People: We dedicate this house.

Pastor:

For the worship of God in prayer, praise, and meditation;

For the proclamation of the everlasting gospel at home,

throughout the nation, and unto the uttermost parts of the earth;

For the preservation in their purity of the sacred ordinances;

People: We dedicate this house.
Pastor:

For the conversion of sinners;
For the perfection of God's people in righteousness;
For the unity in faith and practice of believers;

People: We dedicate this house.
Pastor:

For comfort to those who sorrow and suffer;
For strength to those who are weak;
For Christian fellowship one with another;

People: We dedicate this house.
Pastor:

For sustaining the sacredness of the home;
For instructing and safeguarding the young;
For promoting peace among all peoples;

People: We dedicate this house.
Pastor:

For consolation to the poor;
For healing to the sick;
For hospitality to the stranger;

People: We dedicate this house.
Pastor:

In grateful remembrance of those who have served before us;
In grateful recognition of those who have served with us;
In grateful awareness of the responsibility we bear to those who shall follow us in preparing the way for the return of our Lord;

People: We dedicate this house.

DEDICATORY PRAYER
MUSIC: "Lead On, O King Eternal" (Ernest W. Schurtleff, Henry Smart), by choir and congregation.
BENEDICTION

A Church Building (No. 2)

MEDITATIONS IN MELODY: "Crown Him With Many Crowns" (Matthew Bridges, George J. Elvey), instrumental music.

SCRIPTURE: ". . . Christ also loved the church, and gave himself for it; That he might sanctify and cleanse it with the washing of water by the word, That he might present it to himself a glorious church, not having spot, or wrinkle, or any such thing; but that it should be holy and without blemish" (EPHESIANS 5:25B-27). Read in unison by pastor and congregation.

PRAYER: For an unbroken consciousness of the church as the bride of Christ, and the obligation upon each of its members to keep the church pure in its doctrines and practices until the Lord comes to claim His bride as His own.

MUSIC: "The Church's One Foundation" (Samuel J. Stone, Samuel S. Wesley), by congregation.

Pastor: Before we enter the solemn engagement of dedicating this building to God, we each must first commit our own selves to Him who loved us and who gave Himself for us.

PASTORAL PRAYER (dedication and commitment of pastor and people to the Lord)

MUSICAL RESPONSE: "Amen" (threefold "Amen"), by choir.

Pastor: We dedicate this building to the worship of the one true and living God.

People: "O come, let us worship and bow down: let us kneel before the Lord our maker" (PSALM 95:6).

MUSIC: "O Worship the King" (Robert Grant, Franz Joseph Haydn), by choir and congregation.

Pastor: We dedicate this building to the praise of God.

People: ". . . great is the Lord, and greatly to be praised . . ." (I CHRONICLES 16:25).

MUSIC: "Glory Be to the Father" (Charles Meineke), by choir and congregation.

Pastor: We dedicate this building to fellowship with God through prayer.

People: ". . . our fellowship is with the Father, and with his Son Jesus Christ" (I JOHN 1:3).

MUSIC: " 'Tis the Blessed Hour of Prayer" (Fanny J. Crosby, William H. Doane), vocal arrangement.

Pastor: We dedicate this building to the study of God's Word.

People: "All scripture is given by inspiration of God, and is profitable for doctrine, for reproof, for correction, for instruction in righteousness" (II TIMOTHY 3:16).

MUSIC: "How Firm a Foundation" (George Keith, second tune), by choir.

Pastor: We dedicate this building to Christian fellowship, one with another.

People: ". . . if we walk in the light, as he is in the light, we have fellowship one with another, and the blood of Jesus Christ his Son cleanseth us from all sin" (I JOHN 1:7).

Pastor: We dedicate this building to hospitality to the stranger within our midst.

People: Jesus said, "I was a stranger, and ye took me in" (MATTHEW 25:35).

Pastor: We dedicate this building to ministering to the needs of our own.

People: ". . . let us do good unto all men, especially unto them who are of the household of faith" (GALATIANS 6:10).

Pastor: We dedicate this building to the ministry of meeting human need as far as the power and influence of our personalities and possessions, our time and our talents, our lives and our love can reach.

People: ". . . [Jesus] went about doing good, and healing all that were oppressed of the devil; for God was with him. And we are witnesses of all things which he did . . ." (ACTS 10:38-39).

MUSIC: "Make Me a Blessing" (Ira Wilson, George S. Schuler), by choir.

Pastor: We dedicate this building to the preaching of the gospel.

People: ". . . preach the word, be urgent in season and out of season, convince, rebuke, and exhort, be unfailing in patience and in teaching" (II TIMOTHY 4:2, RSV).

Pastor: We dedicate this building to the spreading of the Good News of salvation to all peoples of all lands.

People: "How then shall they call on him in whom they have not believed? and how shall they believe in him of whom they have not heard? and how shall they hear without a preacher? And how shall they preach, except they be sent? . . ." (ROMANS 10:14-15).

MUSIC: "Here Am I: Send Me" (Daniel March, Wolfgang A. Mozart), vocal arrangement.

Pastor: We dedicate this building to the hastening of the return of our Lord and Saviour, the Shepherd of our souls, the Prince of Peace.

People: "Even so, come, Lord Jesus" (REVELATION 22:21).

PRAYER OF DEDICATION

MUSIC: "All Hail the Power of Jesus' Name" (Edward Perronet, Oliver Holden), choir and congregation.

BENEDICTION

A Religious Education Building

MEDITATIONS IN MELODY: "Zeal, Our Watchword" (Samuel W. Beazley), instrumental music.

CALL TO WORSHIP: ROMANS 9:14, 16, 17.

Program Director: "For as many as are led by the Spirit of God, they are the sons of God."

Response: "The Spirit itself beareth witness with our spirit, that we are the children of God."

In Unison: "And if children, then heirs; heirs of God, and joint-heirs with Christ; if so be that we suffer with him, that we may be also glorified together."

WORSHIP IN PRAYER: That in dedicating this building to God, we wholly commit ourselves to the teaching and leadership of the Holy Spirit.

WORSHIP IN PRAISE: "Blessed Be the Name" (Charles Wesley, B. B. McKinney), by congregation.

WORSHIP IN MEDITATION:

"Ah, that I knew
Where I might find Him!" cried the prophet Job.

This cry as old as man himself
Reflects man's chiefest need: a comradeship with God
     in whom he lives and moves,
And in whose likeness man was made.

Man is no product of capricious chance—
A puppet tossed and torn by tides of circumstance,
Evolving from a senseless mass of energy
Into a thing divine, with grace and dignity;
But having Godlike qualities
He reasons, wills, and loves,
     and finds his highest good
When, knowing God, he moves
On highest levels fashioned for humanity.

Such levels are not won by those who know Him not;
          Or, knowing God,
Deny His right to guide and shape our destinies—
     according to the choices we have made.

The very presence of the God for whom Job cried
Is very real when man, disdainful of self-pride,
     yields unto Him in humble and in childlike trust
His heart, his soul, his strength, his mind;
For in that yielding he will find his Paradise regained:
Work-fellowship with Him who said,
     "Let us make man in our own image";
And in God's likeness man was made.

          —Virginia Ely, "Man's Chiefest Need"

WORSHIP IN DEDICATION:

Program Director: Who presents this building for dedication?
Response: We, the members of this church.

Program Director: For what purpose do we dedicate this building?
Response: That those who come within the teaching ministry
offered here may increase in wisdom, and in favor with God and
man, according to the pattern of growth set for us by Christ, our
Lord.

Program Director: "If we work upon marble it will perish. If we
work upon brass time will efface it. If we rear temples they will
crumble to dust. But if we work upon men's immortal minds, if
we imbue them with high principles, with the just fear of God and
love of their fellow men, we engrave on those tablets something

which no time can efface, and which will brighten and brighten to all eternity" (Daniel Webster).

Response: We dedicate this building for the purpose of providing a place where questing youth may find guidance in moments of decision, through teachers, counselors, and other Christ-like people.

Program Director:

> He stood at the crossroads all alone.
> The sun shone in his face:
> He had no care for the path unknown—
> He was set for a manly race.
> And the road stretched East
> And the road stretched West
> But no one was there to show him the best.
> So the youth turned wrong and went down, down, down
> 'Til he lost the race and the victor's crown,
> And fell at last in an awful snare
> Because no one stood at the crossroads there.
>
> Another youth on another day
> At the self-same crossroads stood;
> He paused awhile to choose the way
> That would lead to the greater good.
> And the road stretched East
> And the road stretched West
> But someone was there to show him the best.
> So this youth went on and on and on
> 'Til he won the race and the victor's crown,
> And came at last to mansions fair
> Because someone stood at the crossroads there.

—Author and Title Unknown

Response: We dedicate this building to those who have any part in the teaching ministry of this church.

Prayer Response (by a teacher):

> Before this class I stand as teacher, Lord;
> I am responsible for them today.
> This is a fearful task, and I am weak;
> Oh, guide me, Father, tell me what to say.
>
> Each pupil has the right to find in me
> A teacher worthy of respect and trust;
> I would not fail this confidence of theirs,
> I would be faithful to them—Lord, I must.

It is the privilege of every one
To look to me for guidance—this I know.
I must be careful lest my feet should stray;
They are so apt to follow where I go.

They listen and believe the things I say,
I pray that thou wilt fill my words with power,
Help me to teach with earnestness and truth,
This is a holy and a sacred hour.

Before this class I stand as teacher, Lord;
Mine is a mighty and God-given task;
No recompense of glory or reward,
But grace to teach aright is all I ask.

—Marjorie McMahan, "A Teacher Prays"

Program Director:

The measure of a teacher's work
Is not what people say,
Nor how much popularity
May come within his day.
It is not in the flash of wit,
Nor play of fancy free,
Nor anything that his own time
Can ever know or see.

The measure of a teacher's work,
Himself can never know.
It is not evident until
The tides have time to flow.
It is the number of the lives
In which he still lives on,
For worth, and right, and happiness,
After his work is done.

—Clarence Edwin Flynn, "The Measure"

PRAYER OF DEDICATION
HYMN OF DEDICATION: "Living for Jesus" (T. O. Chis-
holm, C. Harold Lowdel), by congregation.
BENEDICTION

A Christian Flag

MEDITATIONS IN MELODY: "Loyalty to Christ" (E. T. Cassel, Flora H. Cassel), instrumental music.

MUSIC: "Onward Christian Soldiers" (Sabine Baring-Gould, Arthur S. Sullivan), by congregation.

SCRIPTURE READING: PSALM 145:1, 3-13.

Minister: "I will extol thee, my God, O king; and I will bless thy name for ever and ever."

People: "Great is the Lord, and greatly to be praised; and his greatness is unsearchable."

Minister: "One generation shall praise thy works to another, and shall declare thy mighty acts."

People: "And men shall speak of the might of . . . thy terrible acts: and. . . . They shall abundantly utter the memory of thy great goodness, and shall sing of thy righteousness."

Minister: "The Lord is gracious, and full of compassion; slow to anger, and of great mercy."

People: "The Lord is good to all: and his tender mercies are over all his works."

Minister: "All thy works shall praise thee, O Lord; and thy saints shall bless thee."

People: "They shall speak of the glory of thy kingdom, and talk of thy power; To make known to the sons of men his mighty acts, and the glorious majesty of his kingdom."

Minister: "Thy kingdom is an everlasting kingdom, and thy dominion endureth throughout all generations."

MUSIC: "O God, Our Help in Ages Past" (Isaac Watts, William Croft), by congregation.

Minister: Who presents this Christian flag for dedication?

People: We, the members of ——————————.

Minister: To what purpose do we dedicate this flag?

People: We dedicate this flag as a symbol of our freedom to worship and serve God according to His will, revealed in His Word, as we understand it.

We dedicate this flag as a symbol of our personal dedication and commitment to the preaching of the good tidings of salvation, that sinners may be converted and God's name glorified;

To the healing of broken bodies, bewildered minds, and sin-sick souls;

To the relief of distress among the poor, the aged, the orphaned, the homeless, and the stranger within our gates;

To the building of the spirit of brotherhood among all peoples of all races;

To the propagation and preservation of the gospel of peace throughout the whole world;

To the teaching of the Way, the Truth, and the Life so that all nations may come to bow before Jesus, the Christ of Calvary, and acknowledge Him as King of kings, and Lord of lords.

MUSIC: "Fling Out the Banner" (George W. Doane, John B. Calkin), by congregation; or words may be read with musical accompaniment.

ELEVATION OF CHRISTIAN FLAG

PLEDGE TO THE CHRISTIAN FLAG (given in unison by minister and people):

I pledge allegiance to the Christian flag, and to the Saviour for whose Kingdom it stands, one brotherhood, uniting all mankind in service and love.

PRAYER OF DEDICATION

MUSIC: "Jesus Shall Reign" (Isaac Watts, John Hatten), by congregation.

BENEDICTION

The National Flag

MEDITATIONS IN MELODY: "God of Our Fathers, Whose Almighty Hand" (Daniel C. Roberts, George W. Warren), instrumental music with trumpet accompaniment.

MUSIC: "America, the Beautiful" (Katharine Lee Bates, Samuel A. Ward), by congregation.

SCRIPTURE READING (read responsively by director and people):

Director: ". . . in the name of our God we will set up our banners" (PSALM 20:5).

People: "Thou hast given a banner to them that fear thee . . ." (PSALM 60:4).

Director: "Lift ye up a banner upon the high mountain . . ." (ISAIAH 13:2).

People: "When the enemy shall come in like a flood, the Spirit of the Lord shall lift up a standard against him" (ISAIAH 59:19).

Director: ". . . thou art an holy people unto the Lord thy God . . ." (DEUTERONOMY 7:6).

People: ". . . what nation is there so great, who hath God so nigh unto them, as the Lord our God is in all things that we call upon him for?" (DEUTERONOMY 4:7).

Director: "The Lord did not set his love upon you, nor choose you, because ye were more in number than any people; for ye were the fewest of all people" (DEUTERONOMY 7:7).

People: "Righteousness exalteth a nation . . ." (PROVERBS 14:34).

Director: "Blessed is the nation whose God is the Lord; and the people whom he hath chosen for his own inheritance" (PSALM 33:12).

MUSIC: "God Bless America" (Irving Berlin), by congregation.

PRESENTATION OF FLAG FOR DEDICATION:

Director: Who presents this flag for dedication?

People: We, the people (or name of organization).

Director: For what purpose do we dedicate this flag?

People: We dedicate this flag to the preservation of law and order.

Director: "Let every man remember that to violate the law is to trample on the blood of his father and to tear down the character of his own children's liberty" (Abraham Lincoln).

People: We dedicate this flag to the preservation of the glorious vision which led our forefathers from slavery and oppression into the living light of liberty.

Director: "No nation can live without vision, and no vision will exalt a nation except the vision of real liberty and real justice and purity of conduct" (Woodrow Wilson).

People: We dedicate this flag to the preservation of the dignity of human personality and to the recognition of the right and competency of every individual to approach God in his own way.

Director:

> Our country hath a gospel of her own
> To preach and practice before all the world—
> The freedom and divinity of man,
> The glorious claim of human brotherhood,
> And the soul's fealty to none but God.

> —James Russell Lowell

People: We dedicate this flag to the preservation of our cherished traditions which have given our nation a unique place in world history.

Director: "Our flag symbolizes for us all the beauty and charm and high ideals of our homeland. Its red stands for courage, moral as well as physical. Its white is symbolic of purity, which cannot flourish amidst hate, and fear, and prejudice. Its blue stands for truth and loyalty. Let us then pledge allegiance to our flag with a renewed sense of being loyal every day of our lives. Let us see that everyone in this country gets an equal opportunity to enjoy its privileges" (Jesse H. Holmes).

People: We dedicate this flag to the preservation of those principles of national character which represent the glory of America.

Director:

Not merely in matters material, but in things of the spirit;

Not merely in science, inventions, motors and skyscrapers, but also in ideals, principles, character;

Not merely in the calm assertion of rights, but in the glad assumption of duties;

Not flaunting her strength as a giant, but bending in helpfulness over a sick and wounded world like a good Samaritan;

Not in splendid isolation, but in courageous cooperation;

Not in pride, arrogance, and disdain of other races and peoples, but in sympathy, love and understanding;

Not in treading again the old, worn, bloody pathway which ends inevitably in chaos and disaster, but in blazing a new trail along which, please God, other nations will follow into the New Jerusalem where war shall be no more.

Someday some nation must take that path unless we are to lapse once again into utter barbarism, and that honor we covet for our beloved America.

So, in the spirit and with these hopes we say with all our heart and soul, *America first.*

> —Bishop C. Ashton Oldman

ELEVATION OF THE FLAG

SALUTE TO THE FLAG (by director and people):

I pledge allegiance to the flag of the United States of America and to the republic for which it stands, one nation, under God, indivisible, with liberty and justice for all.

MUSIC: "The Star-Spangled Banner" (Francis Scott Key), instrumental music, one stanza while people continue standing at attention.

PRAYER: "Almighty God, we make our earnest prayer that Thou wilt keep the United States in Thy holy protection; that Thou wilt incline the hearts of the citizens to cultivate a spirit of subordination and obedience to government; to entertain a brotherly affection and love for one another. Amen" (George Washington).

MUSIC: "The Stars and Stripes Forever" (John Philip Sousa), instrumental music, preferably band music.

BENEDICTION

The Home

MEDITATIONS IN MELODY: "Love's Old Sweet Song" (A. Clifton Bingham, J. L. Molloy), instrumental music.

SCRIPTURE READING: I CORINTHIANS 13 (Montgomery Version, or American Standard Version. If Montgomery Version is not available, substitute the word "love" for "charity" in American Standard Version). Read by officiating minister.

Minister: There are only two institutions in society that are of divine origin: the home and the church. The home might be likened to the foundation of a building, and the church to its superstructure. If the foundation of a building be weak, then all of its other members will be unsteady, even unsafe. The sacred records reveal that when God in wisdom and love established the first family on earth, He revealed to them His will concerning an acceptable pattern of worship and devotion, the chief cornerstone of the home. God meant that the first home on earth should be a dedicated home, a home patterned according to His purposes.

Will the members of the family please stand: Before God, and in the presence of these friends, what commitments do you make in dedicating this home to the Lord?

Family (members speaking in unison): We dedicate the conversation of this home to God.

Minister: "Let no evil talk come out of your mouths, but only such as is good for edifying, as fits the occasion, that it may impart grace to those who hear. And do not grieve the Holy Spirit of God, in whom you were sealed for the day of redemption. Let all bitterness and wrath and anger and clamor and slander be put away from you, with all malice, and be kind to one another, tenderhearted, forgiving one another, as God in Christ forgave you. Therefore be imitators of God, as beloved children. And walk in love, as Christ loved us and gave himself up for us, a fragrant offering and sacrifice to God" (EPHESIANS 4:29-5:2, RSV).

Family: We dedicate the work of this home to God.

Minister: ". . . his disciples came to him. And he opened his mouth and taught them, saying: . . . You are the salt of the earth; but if the salt has lost its taste, how shall its saltness be restored? It is no longer good for anything except to be thrown out and trodden under foot by men. You are the light of the world. A city set on a hill cannot be hid. Nor do men light a lamp and put it under a bushel, but on a stand, and it gives light to all in the house. Let your light so shine before men, that they may see your good works and give glory to your Father who is in heaven" (MATTHEW 5:1-2, 13-16, RSV).

Family: We dedicate the teaching ministry of this home to God.

Minister: "Let the word of Christ dwell in you richly in all wisdom; teaching and admonishing one another in psalms and hymns and spiritual songs, singing with grace in your hearts to the Lord. And whatsoever ye do in word or deed, do all in the name of the Lord Jesus, giving thanks to God and the Father by him" (COLOSSIANS 3:16-17).

Family: We dedicate the entertainment in this home to God.

Minister: ". . . test everything; hold fast what is good, abstain from every form of evil. May the God of peace himself sanctify you wholly, and may your spirit and soul and body be kept sound and blameless at the coming of our Lord Jesus Christ" (I THESSALONIANS 5:21-23, RSV).

Family: We dedicate the testimony of this home to God.

Minister: ". . . be strong in the Lord and in the strength of his might. Put on the whole armor of God, that you may be able to stand against the wiles of the devil. For we are not contending against flesh and blood, but against the principalities, against the powers, against the world rulers of this present darkness, against the spiritual hosts of wickedness in the heavenly places. Therefore take the whole armor of God, that you may be able to withstand in the evil day, and having done all, to stand. Stand therefore, having girded your loins with truth, and having put on the breastplate of righteousness, and having shod your feet with the equipment of the gospel of peace; above all taking the shield of faith, with which you can quench all the flaming darts of the evil one. And take the helmet of salvation, and the sword of the Spirit, which is the word of God. Pray at all times in the Spirit, with all prayer and suppli-cation. To that end keep alert with all perseverance, making sup-plication for all the saints . . ." (EPHESIANS 6:10-18, RSV).

MUSIC: "His Way With Thee" (Cyrus S. Nusbaum), vocal arrangement.

PRAYER OF DEDICATION

FAMILY PRAYER (in unison): "God be merciful unto us, and bless us; and cause his face to shine upon us" (PSALM 67:1).

BENEDICTION

A Home in Which There Are Young Children

MEDITATIONS IN MELODY: "Love Is the Theme" (Albert C. Fisher), instrumental music.

MEDITATIONS ON GOD'S WORD: PSALM 19, read in unison by entire assembly, or by a designated reader. (MATTHEW 18:1-6 may be read in unison, if preferred.)

MEDITATIONS IN PRAYER: Praising God and thanking Him for Christian homes.

VOWS OF DEDICATION AND COMMITMENT:

Program Director: Who offers this house for dedication?

Response: We (insert names, such as John and Mary ———).

Program Director: "Except the Lord build the house, they labour in vain that build it . . ." (PSALM 127:1). Before a householder can in spirit and in truth dedicate a house unto the Lord, he must be wholly committed unto the will of the Lord, and must purpose steadfastly in his heart that he will live as completely in the center of that will as the Lord will direct; and by God's grace and guidance, will lead all members of the household to know the Lord and to walk in His way.

Response: ". . . as for me and my house, we will serve the Lord" (JOSHUA 24:15B).

Program Director: "Train up a child in the way he should go: and when he is old, he will not depart from it" (PROVERBS 22:6).

Response by the Father:

> Some things
> Are difficult indeed to say.
> For springs, deep hidden in the heart, well up
> And seem to drown expression.
> If in spite of rising tides one speaks,
> An overflow occurs.
> And words are carried on a flood.
> Many hearing guard themselves, nor heed,
> Excepting when deep answereth to deep.
> But then the words are needless.
>
> This one thing
> A father knows.
> That in the ties of human life,
> A bond, unique, supreme—
> The earthly demonstration
> Of the love of God to men—
> Welds soul to soul the father and his son.
>
> A son of wisdom, says the Word,
> Makes glad the father's heart.
> This is the truth, I know.
> And words cannot express this joy.
> But rising springs, deep in the heart,
> Flow like a river peaceful and serene.

—R. L. Constable, "Hidden Springs"

Program Director or a Designated Reader:

> Lead wisely, father! His small feet will take
>   The path that you are making day by day;
> Adjust your steps to his, and for his sake
>   Lead wisely, father, in the straight, sure Way!

Guide gently, father! In your hands you hold
    A character unformed, and substance rare;
Pure, shining, mobile—it is yours to mold
    The bright beginnings of a structure fair.

Pray daily, father! Hour by precious hour,
    Your building shapes into a man-to-be;
You need that stronger Hand, that higher Power
    To help you build a soul successfully!

Have patience, father, every day will bring
    Its problems, and the need for judgment mild.
You failed today? Tomorrow you may sing;
    Your Father also pitieth His child.

Walk softly, father, let the life unfold
    According to the all-wise Father's plan.
Redeem the time; today is purest gold;
    Tomorrow this small son will be a man!

—Kathryn Blackburn Peck, "Lead Wisely, Father"

Program Director: Homemaking is holy work which must be shared equally by the husband and wife, the parents and children. (Addressed to the wife) Do you join your husband in dedicating this house unto the Lord, and in committing each life in this home to God's guidance and care?

Response by the Wife (Addressed to the husband): "Intreat me not to leave thee, or to return from following after thee: for whither thou goest, I will go; and where thou lodgest, I will lodge: thy people shall be my people, and thy God my God" (RUTH 1:16).

Program Director: When Ruth, the young woman from Moab, made her choice between her gods and her husband's God, her people and her husband's people, it meant for her a separation from everything she had known and loved. Ruth made her decisive declaration, in the beautiful words you have just spoken, because of a priceless possession which was hers—an undivided heart.

It was not given to Ruth to know the glorious end to which her decision would lead. It led her into the ancestral line of her Lord. Today, as you make your vow to the Lord, in the presence of these who are dear to you, you do not know the rewards which await you; but the reward of the faithful shall be yours, and may He ". . . give his angels charge over thee, to keep thee in all thy ways" (PSALM 91:11).

I wash the dirt from little feet,
And as I wash I pray,
"Lord, keep them ever pure and true
To walk the narrow way."
I wash the dirt from little hands,
And earnestly I ask,
"Lord, may they ever yielded be
To do the humblest task."
I wash the dirt from little knees,
And pray, "Lord, may they be
The place where victories are won,
And orders sought from Thee."
I scrub the clothes that soil so soon
And pray, "Lord, may her dress
Throughout eternal ages be
Thy robe of righteousness."

E'er many hours shall pass, I know
I'll wash these hands again;
And there'll be dirt upon her dress
Before the day shall end.
But as she journeys on through life
And learns of want and pain,
Lord, keep her precious little heart
Cleansed from all sin and stain;
For soap and water cannot reach
Where Thou alone canst see.
Her hands and feet, these I can wash—
I trust her heart to Thee.

—Barbara Ryberg, "A Mother's Prayer"

Response (by the mother, if she did not read the above poem; otherwise, by a designated reader) :

God reaches out to homes—the little homes
    Where children pray at night by mother's knees,
And, oh, His heart is warm with tender love,
    His ear made glad to answer each of these!

Their angels sweep the stars in eager flight
    To bear the record up when children pray;
I think that heaven's gates swing wide with joy
    To welcome in the precious things they say!

The incense of a little prayer, slow lisped,
  Repeated word by word from parent tongue,
Is like an alabaster box again
  Of fragrance for the Lord—from one so young.

And what it means to children to be taught
  To seek the Lord, for friendship and for grace?
Ah, that is what eternity will tell
  When we behold their Saviour face to face.

—Hazel Hartwell Simon, "When Children Pray"

Reading: "Home" ("It takes a heap o' livin'") by Edgar A. Guest (available in many books and libraries).

Response by Parents: ". . . let the beauty of the Lord our God be upon us: and establish thou the work of our hands upon us; the work of our hands establish thou it" (PSALM 90:17).

Prayer poem:

> God give us Christian homes!—
> Homes where the Bible is loved and taught,
> Homes where the Master's will is sought,
> Homes crowned with beauty Thy love hath wrought.
> God give us Christian homes!
>
> God give us Christian homes!—
> Homes where the children are led to know,
> Christ in His beauty Who loves them so,
> Homes where the altar fires burn and glow.
> God give us Christian homes!

—B. B. McKinney, "God Give Us Christian Homes"

PRAYER OF DEDICATION (by the family's minister, or a designated friend)

MUSIC: "Love Divine, All Loves Excelling" (Charles Wesley, John Zundel), by family and friends.

BENEDICTION

Note: Since this entire service will not likely be given on any single occasion, material is provided which may be adapted to various occasions. Some poems used may be adapted for broader use by changing the pronouns from singular to plural, or from one gender to the other.

A New Home

MEDITATIONS IN MELODY: "Take Time to Be Holy" (George C. Stebbins), instrumental music.

Minister: "What man is there that hath built a new house, and hath not dedicated it?" (DEUTERONOMY 20:5)

Husband: "Behold, I build an house to the name of the Lord my God, to dedicate it to him . . ." (II CHRONICLES 2:4).

Minister: ". . . the Lord our God is one Lord: And thou shalt love the Lord thy God with all thine heart, and with all thy soul, and with all thy might. And these words, which I command thee this day, shall be in thine heart. And thou shalt teach them diligently unto thy children, and shalt talk of them when thou sittest in thine house, and when thou walkest by the way, and when thou liest down, and when thou risest up. And thou shalt bind them for a sign upon thine hand, and they shall be as frontlets between thine eyes. And thou shalt write them upon the posts of thy house, and on thy gates. . . . Ye shall diligently keep the commandments of the Lord your God, and his testimonies, and his statutes, which he hath commanded thee" (DEUTERONOMY 6:4-9, 17).

Response by Husband: ". . . as for me and my house, we will serve the Lord" (JOSHUA 24:15).

Response by Wife:

> O Thou whose gracious presence blest
>   The home at Bethany,
> This shelter from the world's unrest,
> This home made ready for its Guest
>   We dedicate to Thee.
>
> We build an altar here, and pray
>   That Thou wilt show Thy face.
> Dear Lord, if Thou wilt come to stay,
> This home we consecrate today
>   Will be a holy place.
>
> —Louise F. Benson, "Dedication"

MUSIC: "Home, Sweet Home" (John Howard Payne), vocal arrangement.

Reading:

O happy home, where Thou art loved the dearest,
  Thou loving Friend, and Saviour of our race,
And where among the guests there never cometh
  One who can hold such high and honored place!

O happy home, where two in heart united
  In holy faith and blessed hope are one,
Whom death a little while alone divideth,
  And cannot end the union here begun!

O happy home, where Thou art not forgotten
  When joy is overflowing, full, and free;
O happy home, where every wounded spirit
  Is brought, Physician, Comforter, to Thee—

Until at last, when earth's day's work is ended
  All meet Thee in the blessed home above,
From whence Thou camest, where Thou hast ascended—
  Thy everlasting home of peace and love!

—Karl J. P. Spitta, "O Happy Home"

VOW OF DEDICATION (minister addressing husband and wife, who are standing):

If you this day purpose in your hearts that in consecrating your home unto the Lord you will be faithful in maintaining Christian teachings through your precept and example; training in righteousness through your services in the ministries of your church; godly discipline in your personal habits and in the way of life which you require of all who come beneath your roof; holy conversation; hallowed hospitality; and devotion in your worship of Him to whom you dedicate this house, you will answer in unison: "We will."

PRAYER OF DEDICATION (by minister or designated friend)

MUSIC: "Saviour, Like a Shepherd Lead Us" (William B. Bradbury), by family and friends.

BENEDICTION: "The Lord bless thee and keep thee; The Lord make his face shine upon thee, and be gracious unto thee: The Lord lift up his countenance upon thee, and give thee peace" (NUMBERS 6:24-26).

A Home for Convalescents

MEDITATIONS IN MELODY: "God Will Take Care of You" (C. D. Martin, W. S. Martin), instrumental music.

MUSIC: "All the Way My Saviour Leads Me" (Fanny J. Crosby, Robert Lowry), by congregation.

DEVOTIONAL READING: JOHN 8:1-25, by designated reader.

MUSIC: "Does Jesus Care?" (Frank E. Graeff, L. Lincoln Hall), vocal arrangement.

DEVOTIONAL MEDITATION: During our Lord's earthly ministry, He once said to His disciples, "Come ye yourselves apart into a desert place, and rest a while . . ." (MARK 6:31). The Scriptures explain the reason for this gentle invitation: ". . . there were many coming and going, and they had no leisure so much as to eat" (V. 31B). In our fast-moving age, we too are often too busy to eat, too busy to take sufficient time for rest. The body, as well as the social and spiritual nature of man, cannot endure such situations for very long. We too need our desert places where there is not much activity, where there is room for complete physical rest, where there is opportunity for quiet communion with the Master and meditation on His Word and for seeking to understand His wisdom in planning the way for our life's journey.

We charge our heavenly Father falsely when we hold Him responsible for all the illnesses and misfortunes which befall us. His Word makes it plain that if He so chooses to chastise us, it is but to perfect us in character, that we may be more like him; or it is to keep us from pursuing a way that would lead to our final destruction. Most of our suffering comes upon us by reason of our own violations or some interruption of nature's laws. Whatever the reason for our illnesses, Jesus can turn our hospital rooms into refreshing resting-places where our strength may be renewed, and our spirits may grow strong under the healing power of His presence.

In dedicating this building as a place of rest, recovery, and restoration, we commit ourselves to three meaningful ministries:

First Speaker: We commit ourselves to the ministry of importunate prayer:

> If the shut-ins all united
> In one voice of common prayer,
> What a ceaseless shower of blessing
> Should be falling everywhere!
> Though so weak and ofttimes helpless,
> They can wield a mighty power
> Lifting up their soul's petition
> To the Saviour hour by hour.
> They can importune the Father
> From the "secret place," and then
> In the quiet and the stillness,
> They can hear Him speak to them.
> Never soldier in fierce conflict
> Could a higher honor bring
> Than the shut-in who's performing
> "Secret service" for the King.

—Gertrude Robinson Dugan, "Secret Service"

Christian Herald ran a story concerning Grace Noll Crowell, once the poet laureate of Texas, who has helped to mitigate the suffering in so many hearts through her inspirational writings. It was related that in her young womanhood she suffered a prolonged illness, during which time she might have given up in despair; but "she dipped her pen in prayer and began to write." The Lord graciously restored to Mrs. Crowell her health, and has spared her to bless the lives of multitudes through her ministry of writing.

> Every morning lean thine arms awhile
> Upon the window-sill of heaven
> And gaze upon the Lord;
> Then, with the vision in thy heart,
> Turn strong to meet the day.

—Author Unknown, "Begin the Day with God"

Program Director: ". . . if any man be a worshipper of God, and doeth his will, him he heareth" (JOHN 9:31).

MUSIC: "The Beautiful Garden of Prayer" (Eleanor Allen Schroll, J. W. Fillmore), vocal arrangement.

Second Speaker: We commit ourselves to the ministry of worshipful waiting.

> I saw him stand, his part to smite the drum,
>   Clasping in hand the symbol of his skill;
>   His head uplifted, his shoulders squared, but—still.
> In each appointed place rapt phrases come
> From strings and woodwind, from the brass and reeds.
>   They all with diligence their parts pursue
>   And he who silent is, whose notes are few,
> Is one with them, and stands, and waits—and heeds.
>
> My Master, there are times when I must wait;
>   Thou needest not my single note just now,
>   But my own self Thou needest in my place.
> I will not charge the buffetings of fate;
>   With heart believing and with upturned brow,
>   My score observing—I shall watch Thy face.

—William Marion Runyan, "The Waiting Drummer"

The rests in music are as necessary to the completion of the harmony as are the notes.

Program Director: "Wait on the Lord: be of good courage, and he shall strengthen thine heart: wait, I say, on the Lord" (PSALM 27:14).

Third Speaker: We commit ourselves to the ministry of selfless service. Dr. Frederic Loomis has given us some wise words which apply to us all when we find ourselves in waiting periods, resting times, or desert places. He said, "It's but little good you'll do, watering last year's crops. Yet that is exactly what I have seen hundreds of my patients doing in the past twenty-five years—watering with freely flowing tears things of the irrevocable past. Not the bitter-sweet memories of loved ones, which I could understand, but things done which should not have been done, and things left undone which should have been done.

"I am a doctor, not a preacher; but a doctor, too, must try to understand the joys and sorrows of those who come to him. He should, without preaching, be able to expound the philosophy that one cannot live adequately in the present, nor effectively face the future, when one's thoughts are buried in the past. Moaning over what cannot be helped is a confession of futility and fear, of emotional stagnation—in fact, of selfishness and cowardice. The best way to break this vicious, morbid circle is to stop thinking about yourself, and start thinking about other people. You can lighten your own load by doing something for someone else. By the simple device of doing an outward, unselfish act today, you can make the past recede. The present and future will again take on their true challenge and perspective.

"As a doctor I have seen it tried many, many times and nearly always it has been a far more successful prescription than anything I could have ordered from the drugstore" (*The Best Medicine*).

MUSIC: "Somebody" (John R. Clements, W. S. Weeden), vocal arrangement.

PRAYER OF DEDICATION

BENEDICTION (*by entire assembly*): "Bless the Lord, O my soul: and all that is within me, bless his holy name. Bless the Lord, O my soul, and forget not all his benefits" (PSALM 103:1-2).

A Hospital

MEDITATIONS IN MELODY: "More Love to Thee" (Elizabeth Prentiss, W. H. Doane), instrumental music.

SCRIPTURE READING: MATTHEW 18:1-4, JOHN 13:13-16, MARK 10:43-45, read responsively by director and congregation.

Director: "At the same time came the disciples unto Jesus, saying, Who is the greatest in the kingdom of heaven?"

Congregation: "And Jesus called a little child unto him, and set him in the midst of them, And said, Verily I say unto you, Except ye be converted; and become as little children, ye shall not enter into the kingdom of heaven."

Director: "Whosoever therefore shall humble himself as this little child, the same is greatest in the kingdom of heaven."

Congregation: "Ye call me Master and Lord: and ye say well; for so I am."

Director: "If I then, your Lord and Master, have washed your feet; ye also ought to wash one another's feet. For I have given you an example, that ye should do as I have done to you."

Congregation: "Verily, verily, I say unto you, The servant is not greater than his Lord; neither he that is sent greater than he that sent him."

Director: ". . . but whosoever will be great among you, shall be your minister: And whosoever of you will be the chiefest, shall be servant of all."

Congregation: "For even the Son of man came not to be ministered unto, but to minister, and to give his life a ransom for many."

MUSIC: "Let Others See Jesus in You" (B. B. McKinney), by congregation.

DEVOTIONAL MEDITATION (by a narrator and a reader): We read in MARK 6:56, concerning the healing ministry of our Lord, ". . . as many as touched him were made whole." There were qualities in the touch of the Master which set Him apart from all other healers of His time.

Jesus had a curative touch.

Reader: "And when Jesus was come into Peter's house, he saw his wife's mother laid, and sick of a fever. And he touched her hand, and the fever left her . . ." (MATTHEW 8:14).

Jesus had a compassionate touch.

Reader: "And, behold, two blind men sitting by the way side, when they heard that Jesus passed by, cried out, saying, Have mercy on us, O Lord, thou son of David. . . . So Jesus had compassion on them, and touched their eyes: and immediately their eyes received sight, and they followed him" (MATTHEW 20:30, 34).

Jesus had a conquering touch.

Reader: "Now when he came nigh to the gate of the city, behold, there was a dead man carried out, the only son of his mother, and she was a widow: and much people of the city was with her. And when the Lord saw her, he had compassion on her, and said unto her, Weep not. And he came and touched the bier: and they that bare him stood still. And he said, Young man, I say unto thee, Arise. And he that was dead sat up, and began to speak. And he delivered him to his mother" (LUKE 7:12-15).

Jesus had a cleansing touch.

Reader: "And it came to pass, when he was in a certain city, behold a man full of leprosy: who seeing Jesus fell on his face, and besought him, saying, Lord, if thou wilt, thou canst make me clean. And he put forth his hand, and touched him, saying, I will: be thou clean. And immediately the leprosy departed from him" (LUKE 5:12-13).

Narrator: The touch of Jesus is not only curative, compassionate, conquering, and cleansing, but it has changing power in the bodies, hearts, and lives of men. The only limitation to His power is the limitation of faith and willingness on the part of people to be used as His channels of power in touching those who would be made whole.

Jesus has no feet on which to run errands of mercy but our feet; He has no hands to reach forth in compassionate concern toward the suffering but our hands; He has no minds with which to think thoughts after Him but our minds; and He has no heart through which to love with a giving love, a forgiving love, an everlasting, living love but our hearts.

We have erected this building as a means of ministering to the sick and suffering of our community, and the stranger who needs our care; but the building alone is a cold and voiceless thing. It can go no further in healing human hurts and in meeting human needs than the hands and feet, the minds and hearts of those who serve within these walls are able and willing to go and give.

Director: Who presents this building for dedication?

Response: We, the members of (name of governing group).

Reader:

> From thee all skill and science flow,
>   All pity, care and love,
> All calm and courage, faith and hope;
>   O pour them from above.
>
> And, part them, Lord, to each and all
>   As each and all shall need,
> To rise, like incense, each to thee
>   In noble thought and deed.
>
> And hasten, Lord, that perfect day
>   When pain and death shall cease,
> And thy just rule shall fill the earth
>   With health and light and peace.
>
> —Charles Kingsley, "The Great Physician"

Director: Who offer themselves in full commitment to the service of mankind and the glory of God through their ministry in this hospital?

Response: We, the members of the medical staff and nursing service.

Reader:

> Father, in Thy mysterious presence kneeling,
> > Fain would our souls feel all Thy kindling love;
> For we are weak, and need some deep revealing
> > Of trust and strength and calmness from above.

> Lord, we have wandered forth through doubt and sorrow,
> > And Thou hast made each step an onward one;
> And we will ever trust each unknown morrow;
> > Thou wilt sustain us till its work is done.

> In the heart's depths a peace serene and holy
> > Abides; and when pain seems to have its will,
> Or we despair, O may that peace rise slowly,
> > Stronger than agony, and we be still!

> Now, Father, now, in Thy dear presence kneeling,
> > Our spirits yearn to feel Thy kindling love;
> Now make us strong, we need Thy deep revealing
> > Of trust and strength and calmness from above.

> > > —Samuel Johnson, "Prayer for Strength"

Response: We, the technicians and other employees of this hospital, without whose work its ministry of healing could not be fulfilled, offer our work and ourselves in complete commitment to the service of the Great Physician.

Reader: ". . . they that wait upon the Lord shall renew their strength; they shall mount up with wings as eagles, they shall run, and not be weary; and they shall walk, and not faint" (ISAIAH 40:31).

Response: We, the citizens of this community, commit ourselves to the ministry of healing through our loyalty to the working staff of this hospital and through our support of its mission by our efforts and influence.

Reader:

> At even, when the sun was set,
> > The sick, O Lord, around Thee lay;
> O in what divers pains they met!
> > O with what joy they went away!

> Once more, 'tis eventide, and we,
> > Oppressed with various ills, draw near;
> What if Thy face we cannot see,
> > We know and feel that Thou art here.

O Saviour Christ, our woes dispel;
    For some are sick and some are sad;
And some have never loved Thee well,
    And some have lost the love they had;

And some are pressed with worldly care,
    And some are tried with sinful doubt,
And some such grievous passions tear,
    That only Thou canst cast them out.

And some have found the world is vain,
    Yet from the world they break not free;
And some have friends who give them pain,
    Yet have not sought a friend in Thee;

And none, O Lord, have perfect rest,
    For none are wholly free from sin;
And they who fain would serve Thee best
    Are conscious most of wrong within.

O Saviour Christ, Thou too art Man;
    Thou hast been troubled, tempted, tried;
Thy kind but searching glance can scan
    The very wounds that shame would hide;

Thy touch has still its ancient power;
    No word from Thee can fruitless fall;
Hear, in this solemn evening hour,
    And in Thy mercy heal us all.

—Henry Twells, "At Even When the Sun Was Set"

PRAYER OF DEDICATION
HYMN OF DEDICATION: "Lord, Speak to Me, That I May Speak" (Frances R. Havergal, A. Bost), vocal arrangement.
BENEDICTION: "Lord, thou hast been our dwelling place in all generations. Before the mountains were brought forth, or ever thou hadst formed the earth and the world, even from everlasting to everlasting, thou art God. Let thy work appear unto thy servants, and thy glory unto their children. And let the beauty of the Lord our God be upon us: and establish thou the work of our hands . . ." (PSALM 90:1-2, 16-17).

Note: This service will likely be held in the hospital chapel. Responding groups may approach the altar where they may kneel, or they may kneel in the pews.

A Church Library

MEDITATIONS IN MELODY: "O Zion, Haste" (Mary A. Thomson, James Walch), instrumental music.

SCRIPTURE (by minister and people):

Minister: "So teach us to number our days, that we may apply our hearts unto wisdom" (PSALM 90:12).

People: "The fear of the Lord is the beginning of wisdom . . ." (PSALM 111:10).

Minister: "Length of days is in her right hand, and in her left hand riches and honour" (PROVERBS 3:16).

People: "Her ways are ways of pleasantness, and all her paths are peace" (PROVERBS 3:17).

Minister: "She is a tree of life to them that lay hold upon her: and happy is every one that retaineth her" (PROVERBS 3:18).

People: "The wise shall inherit glory . . ." (PROVERBS 3:35).

Minister: "Wisdom is the principal thing; therefore get wisdom: and with all thy getting get understanding" (PROVERBS 4:7).

People: ". . . wisdom is better than rubies . . ." (PROVERBS 8:11).

Minister: "Exalt her, and she shall promote thee: she shall bring thee to honour, when thou dost embrace her" (PROVERBS 4:8).

MUSIC: "Wonderful Words of Life" (P. P. Bliss), by congregation.

Minister: Who presents this library for dedication?

People: We, the members of this church.

Minister: For what purpose is this library dedicated?

People: We present this library to be dedicated to the glory of God through service to mankind.

Minister: What service shall be performed through this library to redound to man's good and to God's glory?

People: We dedicate this library to the service of little children, to whom our Saviour likened the Kingdom of Heaven, that beautiful seed-thoughts of truth may be planted in their receptive, impressionable minds, leading them into a saving knowledge of the Lord Jesus Christ.

Minister: "Train up a child in the way he should go: and when he is old, he will not depart from it" (PROVERBS 22:6).

People: We dedicate this library to the parents who may use the materials herein as tools in helping their children shape their lives according to the likeness of our Lord who "increased in wisdom and stature, and in favour with God and man" (LUKE 2:52).

Minister: "O Lord, our Lord, how majestic is thy name in all the earth! Thou whose glory above the heavens is chanted by the mouth of babes and infants, thou hast founded a bulwark because of thy foes, to still the enemy and the avenger" (PSALM 8:1-2, RSV).

People: We dedicate this building to the youth, that their zeal may be seasoned with wisdom; that their choices, in all human relationships, may be made in harmony with God's will; and that they may increasingly develop in discernment of the true and the false so that they may be better able to reject the false and accept the true as they advance from youth to maturity.

Minister: "Study to shew thyself approved unto God, a workman that needeth not to be ashamed, rightly dividing the word of truth" (II TIMOTHY 2:15).

People: We dedicate this library to those who are charged with the responsibilities of teaching and training in the various areas of the ministry of this church; that those who are within the realm of their stewardship may develop those attributes which belong to good citizenship, which characterize effective witnessing for our Lord, and which constitute the bases of brotherhood, not only in our own communion but throughout the whole community.

Minister: ". . . by these things men live . . ." (ISAIAH 38:16).

People: We dedicate this library not only to the use of members of this church, but to the edification of all residents who live within the confines of this community, that it may be as a spring of freely-flowing, living water, satisfying minds thirsting for knowledge; as a beacon, set high upon a hill, directing the hearts of all who see it glow in paths of peace, understanding, and good will; and as a vine from which hungry souls may draw sustaining strength and quickening power to walk as Jesus walked, talk as Jesus talked, love as Jesus loved, and live as Jesus lived.

Minister: "Then shall we know, if we follow on to know the Lord . . ." (HOSEA 6:3).

MUSIC: "Open My Eyes, That I May See" (Charles H. Scott), vocal duet or quartet.
PRAYER OF DEDICATION
MUSIC: "Higher Ground" (Johnson Oatman, Jr., Charles H. Gabriel), by congregation.
BENEDICTION

A Public Library

MEDITATIONS IN MELODY: "The Battle Hymn of the Republic" (Julia Ward Howe), instrumental music.
MUSIC: "Faith of Our Fathers" (Frederick W. Faber, H. F. Hemy).
SCRIPTURE READING: PSALM 136:1-9, 26.
Program Director: "O give thanks unto the Lord; for he is good. . . ."
People: ". . . for his mercy endureth for ever."
Program Director: "O give thanks unto the God of gods. . . ."
People: ". . . for his mercy endureth for ever."
Program Director: "O give thanks to the Lord of lords. . . ."
People: ". . . for his mercy endureth for ever."
Program Director: "To him who alone doeth great wonders. . . ."
People: ". . . for his mercy endureth for ever."
Program Director: "To him that by wisdom made the heavens. . . ."
People: ". . . for his mercy endureth for ever."
Program Director: "To him that stretched out the earth above the waters. . . ."
People: ". . . for his mercy endureth for ever."
Program Director: "To him that made great lights. . . ."
People: ". . . for his mercy endureth for ever."
Program Director: "The sun to rule by day. . . ."
People: ". . . for his mercy endureth for ever."
Program Director: "The moon and stars to rule by night. . . ."

People: ". . . for his mercy endureth for ever."
Program Director: "O give thanks unto the God of heaven. . . ."
People: ". . . for his mercy endureth for ever."
PRAYER
Program Director: A popular cookbook contains a chart which gives a list of foods, together with their vitamin contents. The author explains the importance of vitamins in growth processes and in the maintenance of normal health: A prevents eye trouble; B protects nerve tissues; C promotes growth; D promotes calcification, which in turn protects against deformities; G promotes normal nutrition. Without these vitamins, disease and abnormalities may develop.

The library is a repository for educational vitamins, which, if taken properly, promote and protect mental, economic, social, even physical health.

First Speaker: Without vitamin A, one may suffer various eye troubles: nearsightedness—a short look at life—for example. A nearsighted person is not willing to forego the desires of the present for the rewards which adequate training, mature thinking, and good living will yield in the future. One may suffer from farsightedness. He spends his time looking beyond his present opportunities to some far-off day, to a world of unreality where he fancies his dreams will eventually come true, according to some push-button method. Or, one may suffer from color-blindness brought about by prejudices founded on misinformation, or no information. Prevention of these eye troubles may be assured by a regular reading diet which includes philosophy, religion, social science, history, seasoned well with biography and travel.

Second Speaker: Vitamin B is necessary in maintaining good health tone for the nerve tissues. Nerves need to be cushioned against the stress and strain of the Space Age, and other threats to personal welfare which can, if not dealt with properly, produce mental and physical illness. A daily intake of humor, sports, entertainment, and inspirational literature—especially poetry—will assure an adequate supply of vitamin B to meet the needs of most people. Fine arts, if taken for entertainment purposes only, are also rich in vitamin B.

Third Speaker: Vitamin C, which cannot be stored, promotes growth. This vitamin must be taken regularly in order to assure normal health. It is found in all categories of human knowledge, but is especially abundant in the sciences and in applied arts.

Agriculture, architecture, business administration, clinical technology, electronics, engineering, medical sciences, as well as homemaking, animal husbandry, and all of those intriguing studies which are related to crafts and trades, are dependent on vitamin C for their fullest development. Without it the readers will be limited in their expressions of usefulness.

Fourth Speaker: Since deformities may result from a lack of vitamin D, books in the 400 class and the first two divisions of the 500 class must not only be consumed but thoroughly digested. These include the three R's—reading, writing, and arithmetic—along with languages and other branches of mathematics. Without these basic tools of education, one may grow to great stature in certain areas but he will spend much unnecessary time and energy getting from place to place because he does not know that "a straight line is the shortest distance between two points"; and he may endure many frustrations, vexations, and privations as he journeys through life if he does not learn to express himself clearly, concisely, and correctly in both oral and written communications.

Fifth Speaker: Vitamin G promotes normal nutrition. This vitamin is also found in all areas of human knowledge, but rich supplies are available through a basic knowledge of fine arts and literature, and through the regular reading of newspapers and magazines. Strong traces of vitamin G are found in great novels; one rich source, which is often overlooked, is biography: "Lives of great men all remind us, we can make our lives sublime" (Henry Wadsworth Longfellow).

Program Director: One may survive for an indefinite period by eating a single food element, but eventually his appearance and general condition will reveal a state of malnutrition. One may survive emotionally, socially, and economically by reading in only one area—even formula-plot fiction—but his limited scope of reading will likely reveal itself to his disadvantage at some inopportune time. "Reading maketh a full man," said Francis Bacon. The library is a repository for intellectual vitamins which promote good reading for good thinking for good living.

PRAYER OF DEDICATION
MUSIC: The approved state song, or "America."
BENEDICTION

A School Library

MEDITATIONS IN MELODY: "America," instrumental music.

MUSIC: "Battle Hymn of the Republic" (Julia Ward Howe), by congregation.

SALUTE TO THE FLAG (by congregation): "I pledge allegiance to the flag of the United States of America and to the republic for which it stands, one nation, under God, indivisible, with liberty and justice for all."

SCRIPTURE READING: PSALM 111.

Minister: "Praise ye the Lord."

Congregation: "I will praise the Lord with my whole heart, in the assembly of the upright, and in the congregation."

Minister: "The works of the Lord are great, sought out of all them that have pleasure therein."

Congregation: "His work is honourable and glorious: and his righteousness endureth for ever."

Minister: "He hath made his wonderful works to be remembered: the Lord is gracious and full of compassion."

Congregation: "He hath given meat unto them that fear him: he will ever be mindful of his covenant."

Minister: "He hath shewed his people the power of his works, that he may give them the heritage of the heathen."

Congregation: "The works of his hands are verity and judgment; all his commandments are sure."

Minister: "They stand fast for ever and ever, and are done in truth and uprightness."

Congregation: "He sent redemption unto his people: he hath commanded his covenant for ever: holy and reverend is his name."

Minister: "The fear of the Lord is the beginning of wisdom: a good understanding have all they that do his commandments: his praise endureth for ever."

PRAYER: That this library may serve as a fountain of truth and inspiration, enabling its users to advance from knowledge to wisdom and to grow in those essential qualities of citizenship which are valued and cherished by good citizens everywhere. (Prayer may be offered by minister, or member of faculty, school board, or other designated person.)

Minister: Who presents this library for dedication?

Response: We, the people of this community.

Minister: We dedicate this library as a repository of knowledge, truth, and wisdom.

First Reader: Clarence Day said, "The world of books is the most remarkable creation of man. Nothing else that he builds ever lasts. Monuments fall; nations perish; civilizations grow old and die out; and, after an era of darkness, new races build others.

"But in the world of books are volumes that have seen this happen again and again, and yet live on, still young, still as fresh as the day they were written, still telling men's hearts of men centuries dead."

Minister: We dedicate this library as a stimulus to lofty ideals.

Second Reader:

> That book is good which by its silent voice
> Directs me to the shrine of noble thought,
> And urges me to wisely make my choice
> The wheat and not the chaff—this as I ought.
> That book is good which offers me delight
> In simple things, in labor and in rest.
> And if it brings me solace in the night
> When grief is there—that book is blest.
> I shall reread my cherished books again,
> Some new, some legacies of long ago;
> Plumbing their pages for my life's refrain,
> Finding it good; this I have learned and know—
> That book is more than printed pages bound
> Whose substance gives to me a truth profound.

> —Faye Carr Adams, "That Book is Good"

Minister: We dedicate this library as a link which unites the good, the great, and the glorious of the past with the present.

Third Reader:

> "How can you live in Goshen?"
> Said a friend from afar.
> "This wretched country town
> Where folks talk little things all year,
> And plant their cabbage by the moon!"

Said I:
"I do not live in Goshen,—
I eat here, sleep here, work here;
I live in Greece,
Where Plato taught,
And Phidias carved,
And Epictetus wrote.
I dwell in Italy,
Where Michael Angelo wrought
In color, form and mass;
Where Cicero penned immortal lines,
And Dante sang undying songs.
Think not my life is small
Because you see a puny place;
I have my books: I have my dreams;
A thousand souls have left for me
Enchantment that transcends
Both time and place.
And so I live in Paradise,
Not here."

—Edgar Frank, "Goshen"

Minister: We dedicate this library as a handmaiden to the home, the school, and the church in magnifying a quest for learning which has as its chief goal the development of the highest principles of character and good citizenship.

Fourth Reader: "One of our human failings, as I see it, has been our admiration for the 'Middle-of-the-roader.' Certainly many of us agree that the exercise of restraint is one of the marks of the good man. But in some areas compromise is flabby and dangerous. Any person of real conviction and strength must choose one side of the road or the other. It would be a strange kind of education that urged us to be 'relatively' honest, 'sometimes' just, 'usually' tolerant, 'for the most part' decent.

"As you read history and biography, I think you will not come to equate greatness with compromise. Rather, you will find it in decisiveness combined with charity, gentleness, and justice. There will be some wrong decisions, of course, but as long as mistakes are recognized, the loss is far less serious than that occasioned by playing the middle of the road, sitting on the fence, undecided, unconvinced, incapable of strong feeling.

"Life should be a continuing search for those people, those ideas, and those causes to which we can gladly and wholly give ourselves."

—William G. Saltonstall, "Where Do You Stand?"

PRAYER OF DEDICATION
MUSIC: "I Would Be True" (Howard Arnold Walter, Joseph Yates Peek), vocal solo.
BENEDICTION

Table Service for the Lord's Supper

MEDITATIONS IN MELODY: "The Old Rugged Cross" (George Kennard), instrumental music.

WORSHIP IN READING THE WORD OF GOD:

Pastor: In his Letter to the Corinthian Christians, the Apostle Paul said, ". . . I have received of the Lord that which also I delivered unto you, That the Lord Jesus the same night in which he was betrayed took bread: And when he had given thanks, he brake it, and said, Take, eat: this is my body, which is broken for you: this do in remembrance of me. After the same manner also he took the cup, when he had supped, saying, This cup is the new testament in my blood: this do ye, as oft as ye drink it, in remembrance of me" (I CORINTHIANS 11:23-25).

WORSHIP IN MUSIC: "I Gave My Life for Thee" (Frances R. Havergal, P. P. Bliss), by congregation.

WORSHIP IN DEDICATION:

Pastor: In what manner do we share in declaring the Good News of salvation when we observe the ordinance of the Lord's Supper?

People: "For as often as ye eat this bread, and drink this cup, ye do shew the Lord's death till he come" (I CORINTHIANS 11:26).

Pastor: What does this ordinance teach us to remember?

People: ". . . Christ died for our sins according to the scriptures" (I CORINTHIANS 15:3).

Pastor: Is the death of Jesus sufficient for the atonement of all people of all times?

People: ". . . he died for all, that they which live should not henceforth live unto themselves, but unto him which died for them, and rose again" (II CORINTHIANS 5:15).

Pastor: What are we to remember concerning our sins?

People: ". . . the blood of Jesus Christ his Son cleanseth us from all sin" (1 JOHN 1:7).

Pastor: What are we to remember concerning our relationship to God through the death of His Son?

People: ". . . we were reconciled to God by the death of his Son . . ." (ROMANS 5:10).

Pastor: What are we to remember concerning our Saviour's death?

People: ". . . Christ also hath once suffered for sins, the just for the unjust, that he might bring us to God, being put to death in the flesh, but quickened by the Spirit" (1 PETER 3:18).

Pastor: What are we to remember concerning the burial of our Lord?

People: ". . . he was buried, and . . . he rose again the third day . . ." (1 CORINTHIANS 15:4).

Pastor: What are we to remember concerning His resurrection?

People: ". . . he which raised up the Lord Jesus shall raise up us also by Jesus . . ." (II CORINTHIANS 4:14).

Pastor: What are we to remember concerning His ascension into heaven?

People: ". . . he was taken up; and a cloud received him out of their sight. And while they looked stedfastly toward heaven as he went up, behold, two men stood by them in white apparel; Which also said, Ye men of Galilee, why stand ye gazing up into heaven? this same Jesus, which is taken up from you into heaven, shall so come in like manner as ye have seen him go into heaven" (ACTS 1:9B-11).

Pastor: What are we to remember concerning His triumph over sin, death, and the grave?

People: "O death, where is thy sting? O grave, where is thy victory? The sting of death is sin; and the strength of sin is the law. But thanks be to God, which giveth us the victory through our Lord Jesus Christ" (1 CORINTHIANS 15:55-57).

MUSIC: "When I Survey the Wondrous Cross" (Isaac Watts, Lowell Mason), vocal arrangement.

Pastor: Who presents these sacred vessels with which we commemorate the atoning death of our blessed Lord?

People: We who are members of His church, His beloved bride.

Pastor: We dedicate these cups and these plates for use in serving the memorial service of our Lord. He has ordained that as often as we partake of the elements used in this service, the broken bread will remind us of His broken body; and the wine—crushed from the fruit of the vine—will remind us of His shed blood. In dedicating these vessels to our Saviour's service and glory, may this be an occasion when we who are redeemed from sin, and cleansed from sin by His blessed blood, may commit ourselves anew to the holy service of faithfully proclaiming that ". . . he is able also to save them to the uttermost that come unto God by him, seeing he ever liveth to make intercesssion for them" (Hebrews 7:25).

MEDITATION:

> Above the hills of time the Cross is gleaming,
>   Fair as the sun when night has turned to day;
> And from it love's pure light is richly streaming,
>   To cleanse the heart and banish sin away.
> To this dear Cross the eyes of men are turning
>   To-day as in the ages lost to sight;
> And for the love of Christ men's hearts are yearning
>   As shipwrecked seamen yearn for morning light.
>
> The cross, O Christ, Thy wondrous love revealing,
>   Awakes our hearts as with the light of morn,
> And pardon o'er our sinful spirits stealing
>   Tells us that we, in Thee, have been re-born.
> Like echoes to sweet temple bells replying,
>   Our hearts, O Lord, make answer to Thy love;
> And we will love Thee with a love undying,
>   Till we are gathered to Thy home above.
>
> —Thomas Tiplady, "Above the Hills of time"

PRAYER OF DEDICATION
MEMORIAL SUPPER
MUSIC: "Jesus, Keep Me Near the Cross" (Fanny J. Crosby, W. H. Doane), by congregation.
BENEDICTION

A Mission Building

MEDITATIONS IN MELODY: "Let the Lower Lights Be Burning" (P. P. Bliss), instrumental music.

CALL TO WORSHIP: MATTHEW 28:18-20.

Program Director: "And Jesus came and spake unto them, saying, All power is given unto me in heaven and in earth."

Congregation: "Go ye therefore, and teach all nations, baptizing them in the name of the Father, and of the Son, and of the Holy Ghost: Teaching them to observe all things whatsoever I have commanded you: and, lo, I am with you alway, even unto the end of the world. Amen."

MUSIC: "Rescue the Perishing" (Fanny J. Crosby, W. H. Doane), by congregation.

DEVOTIONAL MEDITATION: "Missions, Our Mission."

Just before our Lord's return to heaven, in His last recorded visit with His followers, He said, ". . . it behoved Christ to suffer, and to rise from the dead the third day: And that repentance and remission of sins should be preached in his name among all nations, beginning at Jerusalem. And ye are witnesses of these things" (LUKE 24:46-48).

Christ, our Lord, taught through His words and His work while He was here the area of our responsibility in soul winning. He made it plain that missions—telling the sweet story of redeeming love —are the mission of every Christian. Even though the scope of our responsibilities and activities must extend around the world, we are to begin at Jerusalem, our home base. In building and dedicating this mission, we are committing ourselves to a program of seeking and winning those members of society who might never be won through the regular operations of our organizational activities in the church. They will not come to the church seeking salvation; the church, through its ministry in missions, must go in search of them with the message of salvation.

We are to seek the outcasts of society. Jesus broke three social customs when He sat on Jacob's well one day and had conversation with a woman. The woman was a Samaritan, a half-caste, and the Jews had no dealings with the Samaritans. The woman was an outcast, a woman without character, a woman with whom people of high social standing would not have fellowship. Also, it was contrary to social custom for an oriental woman to engage in conversation with men in public places. Our Lord's disciples marveled that He would violate the sanctions of society in such manner. Our Saviour looked beyond all social barriers and saw a soul who was thirsty for water which He alone could give; and the woman left the well to go into the city as a messenger of salvation to her former associates in sin. Jesus came to save the outcasts of society; we are His witnesses unto them. (See JOHN 4:1-30.)

We are to seek the lost who may be living within the shadow of the church. Two of our Lord's disciples, Peter and John, who had learned well what Jesus would have done in such circumstances, went to the Temple to pray. As they approached the gate, a man who had been lame from birth asked them for financial help. Peter fastened his eyes on the man, commanded the man to look on them, then gave his startling reply: "Silver and gold have I none; but such as I have give I thee: In the name of Jesus Christ of Nazareth rise up and walk" (ACTS 3:6). For years the crippled man had been laid at the gate of the temple daily that he might beg for charity. For years worshipers who were going to the temple to pray had passed by him, probably many of them giving to him the thing for which he asked; but he remained a cripple, a charge on society. When the two stalwart men of God came by, they had not that to give for which the cripple cried, but through a marvelous manifestation of God's grace they had that to give which he needed most —strength to stand on his own feet. When, in the name of Jesus Christ, they had imparted to him God's gift, he was no longer a beggar, a charge on society, a cripple who sat outside the temple gate; he became a citizen of whom society could be proud, and took his place inside the temple with other worshipers, praising God and bearing glorious testimony concerning the grace of God which frees all men from whatever may limit or restrict them in serving God.

In every hamlet, in every city, in every countryside, there are people living within the shadow of the church who will never come within the church building itself to hear the Word preached. They are passed by every day by people who should have a care for their souls; but no one ever stops and tries to relieve them of the infirmities which keep them bound by the restrictions of sin. They must be found; they must be quickened with new life through the power of the gospel. Someone must realize that without a saving knowledge of Jesus Christ these people are lost; they will remain in their helplessness, and will die in their sinful state.

This mission which we dedicate today is built for the purpose of finding those who are so sick with sin that they cannot find the door of salvation unless someone will guide them, and in the name of Jesus Christ will lead them into a healing, transforming experience through a knowledge of the glorious gospel of the Son of God. We are His witnesses.

We are to seek the ones who are religious but who do not have a saving knowledge of Christ our Lord. The angel of the Lord appeared to Philip and directed him to go from Jerusalem to Gaza. As he journeyed he met a lone traveler, an official in the court of the Queen of Ethiopia. Philip was directed by the Spirit to join the man in the chariot. The Bible reveals the significant fact that Philip did not argue with the Lord, but "ran thither to him," and he found the Ethiopian—an earnest seeker for the truth—reading a passage from Isaiah which describes the suffering Saviour. Beginning with the same Scripture, Philip told him the Good News about Jesus, and he led the seeker into a personal acceptance of the Christ of Calvary as his Saviour.

Philip was directed by the Spirit of the Lord to talk to a man about the only way God has provided for men to be saved. The man to whom Philip was directed was devoutly religious; he had been to Jerusalem on a religious pilgrimage; he was reading the Bible; he was as sincere as a man could be; but he did not have a saving knowledge of Jesus as the Lamb of God.

This area of evangelism represents one of the hardest to approach; but there are people all around us who are seeking to enter the door of salvation through some way other than repentance toward God and faith in the Lord Jesus Christ. The Word says ". . . I say unto you, He that entereth not by the door into the sheepfold, but climbeth up some other way, the same is a thief and a robber" (JOHN 10:1). These people represent an area of our responsibility. We are our Lord's witnesses unto them.

If our civilization survives, we must bind together all peoples of all segments of society with the all-embracing cohesive of redeeming love—the one means of communication and coordination which transcends all language, social, cultural, and economic barriers.

Chained to the Roman soldier in his room,
Dank from the Tiber's overflowing tide,
The old apostle sat in the half-lit gloom.
He saw his guard, shivering, gather the wide
Folds of his long, warm cloak about him tight,
Fasten it closely over all he wore.
And as he gazed on this familiar sight,
It gave a meaning never caught before.
"Dearly beloved," cramped fingers wrote with care,
"Be clothed with tenderness, humility,
With gentle spirit, ready to forebear,
Forgiving as the Lord has pardoned thee.
Put over all, for calm or stormy weather,
The cloak of love, that fastens all together."

—Belle Chapman Morrill, "The Cloak of Love"

Program Director: Who offers this building for dedication?

Response: We, the (name of governing group).

Program Director: For what purpose do we dedicate this building?

Response: That the poor may have the gospel preached to them.

Program Director: ". . . the gift of God is eternal life through Jesus Christ our Lord" (ROMANS 6:23).

Response: That those dead in trespasses and sin may be quickened to new life.

Program Director: "The Lord thy God in the midst of thee is mighty; he will save, he will rejoice over thee with joy . . ." (ZEPHANIAH 3:17).

Response: That those who hunger and thirst after righteousness may be filled.

Program Director: "He that goeth forth and weepeth, bearing precious seed, shall doubtless come again with rejoicing, bringing his sheaves with him" (PSALM 126:6).

Response: That this building may serve as a beacon light wherein Christ's witnesses may direct the lost and erring unto Him.

Program Director: ". . . they that be wise shall shine as the brightness of the firmament; and they that turn many to righteousness as the stars for ever and ever" (DANIEL 12:3).

Response: That the name of God may be glorified in every heart and in every home within the radius of this mission's influence.

Program Director: ". . . ye shall know that the living God is among you . . ." (JOSHUA 3:10).

PRAYER OF DEDICATION

MUSIC: "Jesus Saves" (Priscilla J. Owens, William J. Kilpatrick), by congregation.

BENEDICTION: "Blessing, and glory, and wisdom, and thanksgiving, and honour, and power, and might, be unto our God for ever and ever. Amen" (REVELATION 7:12).

An Organ

MEDITATIONS IN MELODY: "O for a Thousand Tongues" (Charles Wesley, Carl G. Glaser), instrumental music.

MUSIC: "Praise, My Soul, the King of Heaven" (Henry F. Lyte, Henry Smart), by congregation.

DEVOTIONAL MEDITATION: "Music is the harmonious voice of creation; an echo of the invisible world; one note of the divine concord which the entire universe is destined one day to sound" (Guiseppe Mazzini).

Several years ago a newspaper printed the following story under the caption, "I Am Music" (the source of the story the paper was not able to verify):

A supervisor of music in a public school was approached by a seventh-grade boy, who said to him: "I found something about music in an old paper that I like very much. I thought you would like it too." The boy handed the teacher a crumpled newspaper clipping which contained this beautiful tribute to music:

"Servant and master am I; servant of those dead and master of those living. Through me, spirits immortal speak the message that makes them nearby. I make the world weep and laugh, wonder and worship.

"I tell the story of love, the story of hate, the story that saves and the story that destroys. I am the incense upon which prayers float to Heaven. I am the smoke which palls over the field of battle where men die with me on their lips.

"I am close to the marriage altar and when the grave opens I stand nearby. I call the wanderer home, I rescue the soul from the depths, I open the lips of lovers and through me the dead whisper to the living.

"One I serve as I serve all, and the king I make my slave as easily as I subject his slave. I speak through the birds of the air, the insects of the field, the crash of waters on rock-ribbed shores, the sighing of wind in the trees, and I am even heard by the soul that knows me in the clatter of wheels on city streets. I am music!"

VOWS OF DEDICATION AND COMMITMENT:

Director: We dedicate this organ that the name of the Lord God Almighty may be glorified through the messages of music and with songs of praise.

Response: "Praise ye the Lord. Praise God in his sanctuary: praise him in the firmament of his power. Praise him for his mighty acts: praise him according to his excellent greatness. Praise him with the sound of the trumpet: praise him with the psaltery and harp. Praise him with the timbrel . . . : praise him with stringed instruments and organs. Praise him upon the loud cymbals: praise him upon the high sounding cymbals. Let every thing that hath breath praise the Lord. Praise ye the Lord" (PSALM 150).

MUSIC: "Glorious Is Thy Name" (B. B. McKinney), choral arrangement.

Director: We dedicate this organ that our Lord may be glorified with songs of thanksgiving.

Response: "Let us come into his presence with thanksgiving; let us make a joyful noise to him with songs of praise!" (PSALM 95:2 RSV).

MUSIC: "Anniversary Hymn" (Edward Hughes Pruden, Edward Kremser), by congregation.

Director: We dedicate this organ that through inspirational music the hearts of those who hear may be attuned more perfectly to the will of God, and that lives may be keyed more perfectly to His Word.

Response: "Then shall we know, if we follow on to know the Lord . . ." (HOSEA 6:3).

MUSIC: "Open My Eyes, That I May See" (Clara H. Scott), vocal arrangement.

Director: We dedicate this organ that the story of redeeming love may be proclaimed through instrumental music and spiritual songs.

Response: "We love him, because he first loved us" (1 JOHN 4:19).

MUSIC: "I Know Whom I Have Believed" (Daniel W. Whittle, James McGranahan), vocal arrangement.

Director: We dedicate this organ that sinners may be converted and that our Lord's wayfaring children may be drawn into a closer walk with Him.

Response: "The Spirit of the Lord God is upon me; . . . to give unto them beauty for ashes, the oil of joy for mourning, the garment of praise for the spirit of heaviness . . ." (ISAIAH 61:1-3).

MUSIC: "Nearer, My God, to Thee" (Sarah F. Adams, Lowell Mason), vocal arrangement.

READING:

> Rejoice and sing unto the mighty Lord,
>   For praise is comely for an upright man;
> If we have tuned our hearts to seek His word
>   Are we then Pharisee or Publican?
> For simple gifts, let our hearts speak their praise;
>   The needled rain, piercing the thirsty ground;
> For nights to rest; the sun's bright warming rays;
>   And mockingbirds whose lilting songs abound.
> Who has not felt the courage in a smile?
>   It speaks far more than words when we are sad;
> Somewhere upon each long and lonely mile
>   A friend will grip our hand and make us glad.
> Rejoice and sing—for these are gifts from God,
>   Our hearts, in truth, are a divining rod.

> —Faye Carr Adams, "Rejoice and Sing"

PRAYER OF DEDICATION

MUSIC: "To God Be the Glory" (Fanny J. Crosby, W. H. Doane), by congregation.

BENEDICTION

A Prayer Chapel

MEDITATIONS IN MELODY: "Whisper a Prayer" (Scott Lawrence), instrumental music.

MUSIC: " 'Tis the Blessed Hour of Prayer" (Fanny J. Crosby, W. H. Doane), by congregation.

SCRIPTURE READING (read responsively by director and congregation):

Director: "Seek the Lord and his strength, seek his face continually" (I CHRONICLES 16:11).

Congregation: ". . . in the shadow of thy wings will I make my refuge . . ." (PSALM 57:1).

Director: "Blessed is the man that heareth me, watching daily at my gates, waiting at the posts of my doors" (PROVERBS 8:34).

Congregation: ". . . let us kneel before the Lord our maker" (PSALM 95:6).

Director: "Be not rash with thy mouth, and let not thine heart be hasty to utter any thing before God: for God is in heaven, and thou upon earth: therefore let thy words be few" (ECCLESIASTES 5:2).

Congregation: ". . . if any man be a worshipper of God, and doeth his will, him he heareth" (JOHN 9:31).

Director: "Ask, and it shall be given you; seek, and ye shall find; knock, and it shall be opened unto you" (MATTHEW 7:7).

Congregation: ". . . the same Lord over all is rich unto all them that call upon him" (ROMANS 10:12).

Director: "If ye abide in me, and my words abide in you, ye shall ask what ye will, and it shall be done unto you" (JOHN 15:7).

Congregation: "The effectual fervent prayer of a righteous man availeth much" (JAMES 5:16).

Director: ". . . his ears are open unto their prayers . . ." (I PETER 3:12).

Congregation: ". . . whatsoever we ask, we receive of him, because we keep his commandments, and do those things that are pleasing in his sight" (I JOHN 3:22).

Director: "Pray without ceasing" (I THESSALONIANS 5:17).

Congregation: "I will pray with the spirit, and I will pray with the understanding . . ." (I CORINTHIANS 14:15).

Director: ". . . where two or three are gathered together in my name, there am I in the midst of them" (MATTHEW 18:20).

MUSIC: "Sweet Hour of Prayer" (W. W. Walford, William B. Bradbury), by congregation.

POEM:

> Out of the peace and quiet of an hour
> Alone with God may come a wealth so great
> That any heart can find a hidden power
> Undreamed of hitherto: the power to wait
> His blessed will, or power to rise and go
> Into the hard-pressed battle for the right;
> Or it can give the impetus to grow
> Out of hindering darkness into the light.
> As Christ Himself felt deep and vital need
> Of many a quiet waiting while alone
> With God the Father, who has food to feed
> All hunger that the heart has ever known;
> So we should seek Him, day by passing day,
> In the deep solitude of some still place,
> And learn from Him the high and holy way
> Of peace and patience, charity and grace.

—Grace Noll Crowell, "The Quiet Hour"

MUSIC: "Did You Think to Pray?" (M. A. Kidder, W. O Perkins), vocal arrangement.

PRAYER OF DEDICATION

MUSIC: "My Prayer" (P. P. Bliss), by congregation.

BENEDICTION (by congregation): "I love the Lord, because he hath heard my voice and my supplications. Because he hath inclined his ear unto me, therefore will I call upon him as long as I live" (PSALM 116:1-2).

A Public School Building

MEDITATIONS IN MELODY: "America, the Beautiful" (Katharine Lee Bates, Samuel A. Ward), instrumental music.

PRAYER (for an awareness of God's guidance and benediction)

PLEDGE TO THE FLAG (see *Dedication of American Flag*)

NATIONAL ANTHEM: "The Star-Spangled Banner" (Francis Scott Key), chorus or instrumental music.

SCRIPTURE READING: ECCLESIASTES 12:1-7, 13.

Program Director: Rabindranath Tagore is reported to have said that "Every time a child is born, it shows that God has not lost faith in human nature." The erection of this building is a manifestation of faith on the part of the citizens of this community in human nature. It is a manifestation of faith, not only in the present, but in unborn generations in whose keeping the progress and welfare of our society must rest. Not only is this building a manifestation of our faith in our youth of today, and in those who will follow; it is a manifestation of our wise concern for their mental, moral, and social development and guidance.

The great educator, George Peabody, once said, "Education is a debt due from the present to the future generations." This building represents a meaningful step toward making possible for all children who live or shall live within the radius of the teaching ministry of this school to so develop their latent abilities that they may be to them as tools with which they may carve out lives that will be sustaining satisfactions to them, a benefaction to this community, and a bulwark against those forces which may now or in times to come threaten our way of life which is so cherished by every right-thinking American.

The great of all ages have placed much stress on the value of education. It was the writer of the Proverbs in the Bible who said, ". . . as he [a man] thinketh in his heart, so is he" (PROVERBS

23:7). If a man thinks right, he is right. Right teaching is the first aid in right thinking.

Let us have a roll call of some of the great thinkers, from medieval to modern times, and learn from them the value they placed on education.

Publilius Syrus, a Latin who lived during the first century before Christ, what is your opinion as to the value of education?

Reader: "It is only the ignorant who despise education."

Director: Seneca, the philosopher?

Reader: "As the soil, however rich it may be, cannot be productive without culture, so the mind without cultivation can never produce good fruits."

Director: William Shakespeare?

Reader: "The common curse of mankind—folly and ignorance."

Director: Joseph Addison, great writer of great poetry?

Reader: "What sculpture is to a block of marble, education is to the human soul. The philosopher, the saint, the hero, the wise and the good, or the great, very often lie hid and concealed in a plebeian, which a proper education might have disinterred and brought to light."

Director: Benjamin Franklin, one of the greatest of our American thinkers?

Reader: "If a man empties his purse in his head, no man can take it away from him."

Director: Thomas Cooper, English political reformer and religious leader?

Reader: "Neither piety, virtue, nor liberty can long flourish in a community where the education of youth is neglected."

Director: James Russell Lowell?

Reader: "It was in making education not only common to all, but in some sense compulsory to all, that the destiny of the free republic of America was practically settled."

Director: John Ruskin?

Reader: "Education does not mean teaching people to know what they do not know; it means teaching them to behave as they do not behave."

Director: Thomas Huxley?

Reader: "Perhaps the most valuable result of all education is the ability to make yourself do the thing you have to do when it ought to be done, whether you like it or not; it is the first lesson which ought to be learned, and, however early a man's training begins, it is probably the last lesson he learns thoroughly."

Director: Dr. Charles William Eliot, educator and former president of Harvard University?

Reader: "Liberal education develops a sense of right, duty and honor; and more and more in the modern world, large business rests on rectitude and honor as well as on good judgment."

Director: Dr. Nicholas Murray Butler, first president of the Industrial Education Association (which later became Teachers College of Columbia University)?

Reader: "There are five tests of the evidences of education—correctness and precision in the use of the mother tongue; refined and gentle manners, the result of fixed habits of thought and action; sound standards of appreciation of beauty and of worth, and, a character based on these standards; power and habit of reflection; efficiency or the power to do."

Director: Ramsay MacDonald, English statesman?

Reader: "The educated man is a man with certain spiritual qualities which make him calm in adversity, happy when alone, just in his dealings, rational and sane in the fullest meaning of that word in all the affairs of life."

Director: Franklin Delano Roosevelt?

Reader: "Every student must be a volunteer in the intellectual and spiritual struggle to preserve freedom for mankind."

Director: Dr. James Bryant Conant, former president of Harvard University, has spoken a most timely word for us to remember:

Reader: "A democracy can only be strong if all the citizens are properly educated and careers are freely open to all the talented."

Director: Who presents this building for dedication?

People: We, the citizens of this community.

Director: With what purpose do we dedicate this building?

People: We dedicate this building to the advancement of liberal and vocational education; to the discovery and development of latent abilities; the growth and guidance of mental faculties; the cultivation of high principles of character; the teaching of a true sense of values; the awakening and nurturing of an appreciation of real beauty; the training in good citizenship; and to instructions and participations in practices which represent Americanism at its best.

PRAYER OF DEDICATION
MUSIC: "America," by congregation.
BENEDICTION

Trees

MEDITATIONS IN MELODY: "Trees" (Joyce Kilmer), instrumental music.

CALL TO WORSHIP:

Director: "In the beginning God created the heaven and the earth" (GENESIS 1:1).

People: "And God said, Let the earth bring forth grass, the herb yielding seed, and the fruit tree yielding fruit after his kind, whose seed is in itself, upon the earth . . ." (GENESIS 1:11).

DEVOTIONAL MEDITATION: Two of God's purposes in creating trees are set forth in GENESIS 2:9: ". . . out of the ground made the Lord God to grow every tree that is pleasant to the sight, and good for food. . . ." God made trees to grow so that they might beautify the earth and share in affording life-sustaining food for man and beast, even the smallest of animal life. As is true of all God's blessings, the benefits of His trees are not confined within the narrow scope of defined purpose, but pour out in measureless benefits into other areas.

The following lines are said to have been found posted on a tree in a park in Seville, Spain:

> Ye who pass by and would raise your hand against me,
> Hearken ere you harm me!
> I am the heat of your hearth on the cold winter nights,
> The friendly shade screening you from summer sun.
> My fruits are refreshing drafts,
> Quenching your thirst as you journey on.
> I am the beam that holds your home,
> The board of your table,
> The bed on which you lie,
> And the timber that builds your boat.
> I am the handle of your hoe,

The door of your homestead,
The wood of your cradle,
And the shell of your coffin.
I am the bread of kindness, and the flower of beauty.
Ye who pass by, listen to my prayer: harm me not.

—Author and Title Unknown

As we dedicate these trees today, let us be reminded of the sacred places of commitment and dedication in which trees have served. It was beneath the trees that our Master won His last victory over Satan when He prayed, ". . . nevertheless not my will, but thine, be done" (LUKE 22:42); it was on a tree that He completed the twofold purpose which brought Him into the world: ". . . that they might have life, and . . . have it more abundantly" (JOHN 10:10); and ". . . to seek and to save that which was lost" (LUKE 19:10).

MUSIC: "Into the Woods My Master Went" (Sidney Lanier, Peter C. Lutkin), vocal arrangement.

Director: May these trees which we dedicate today ever serve to stimulate those who view their beauty, rest within their shade, or find refuge beneath their sheltering branches, with the spirit of rededication of the entire self in selfless service to mankind, and to the glory of the Maker.

MUSIC: "I Saw God Wash the World Last Night" (William L. Stidger, George Shackley).

PRAYER OF DEDICATION

MUSIC: "For the Beauty of the Earth" (Folliott S. Pierpoint, Conrad Kocher), vocal arrangement.

BENEDICTION

A Youth Center

MEDITATIONS IN MELODY: "Living for Jesus" (T. O. Chisholm, C. Harold Lowden), instrumental music.

SCRIPTURE READING:

       PROVERBS 3:1-12, RSV, read by a young man.

       PROVERBS 31:10-31, read by young woman.

MUSIC: "Give of Your Best to the Master" (Mrs. Charles Barnard), by choir and congregation.

Minister: For what purpose do we dedicate this building?

People: We dedicate this building that the youth of this community may be taught the living truth as revealed in God's Word, and that they may learn to walk in obedience to His commands in the spirit of love and gladness.

Minister: "Train up a child in the way he should go: and when he is old, he will not depart from it" (PROVERBS 22:6).

Response by a Young Man:

O young and fearless Prophet of ancient Galilee,
Thy life is still a summons to serve humanity,
To make our thoughts and actions less prone to please the crowd,
To stand with humble courage for Truth with hearts uncowed.

We marvel at the purpose that held Thee to Thy course,
While ever on the hilltop before Thee loomed the cross;
Thy steadfast face set forward where love and duty shone,
While we betray so quickly and leave Thee there alone.

O young and fearless Prophet, we need Thy presence here,
Amid our pride and glory to see Thy face appear;
Once more to hear Thy challenge above our noisy day,
Again to lead us forward along God's holy way.

                    —S. Ralph Harlow, "O Young and Fearless Prophet"

People: We dedicate this building that our youth may be taught to assume responsibilities for proclaiming the glad tidings of salvation, both at home and unto the remotest island of the sea.

Minister: "How beautiful are the feet of them that preach the gospel of peace, and bring glad tidings of good things!" (ROMANS 10:15B).

People: We dedicate this building that our youth may be instructed in the doctrines of the church.

Minister: "All scripture is given by inspiration of God, and is profitable for doctrine, for reproof, for correction, for instruction in righteousness: That the man of God may be perfect, throughly furnished unto all good works" (II TIMOTHY 3:16-17).

People: We dedicate this building that our youth may be nurtured in all things which pertain to growth in Christlikeness.

Minister: "That Christ may dwell in your hearts by faith; that ye, being rooted and grounded in love, May be able to comprehend with all saints what is the breadth, and length, and depth, and height; And to know the love of Christ, which passeth knowledge, that ye might be filled with all the fulness of God" (EPHESIANS 3:17-19).

Response by a Young Woman:

> Almighty Lord, with one accord
> We offer Thee our youth,
> And pray that Thou wouldst give us now
> The warfare of the truth.
>
> Thy cause doth claim our souls by name,
> Because that we are strong;
> In all the land, one steadfast band,
> May we to Christ belong.
>
> * * * *
>
> Our hearts be ruled, our spirits schooled
> Alone Thy will to seek;
> And when we find Thy blessed mind,
> Instruct our lips to speak.
>
> —M. Woolsey Stryker, "Almighty Lord, with One Accord"

People: We dedicate this building that youth may grow in a vital awareness of the sacredness of life and the sanctity of the body as the temple of the Holy Spirit.

Minister: ". . . know ye . . . that . . . ye are not your own?

For ye are bought with a price: therefore glorify God in your body, and in your spirit, which are God's" (1 CORINTHIANS 19B-20).

People: We dedicate this building that youth may be developed in the graces of Christian fellowship.

Minister: "And let the peace of God rule in your hearts, to the which also ye are called in one body; and be ye thankful. And whatsoever ye do in word or deed, do all in the name of the Lord Jesus, giving thanks to God and the Father by him" (COLOSSIANS 3:15, 17).

Reader (an adult member):

> How beautiful is youth! how bright it gleams
> With its illusions, aspirations, dreams!
> Book of Beginnings, Story without End,
> Each maid a heroine, and each man a friend!

*   *   *   *

> All possibilities are in its hands;
> No danger daunts it, and no foe withstands;
> In its sublime audacity of faith,
> "Be thou removed!" it to the mountain saith,
> And with ambitious feet, secure and proud,
> Ascends the ladder leaning on the cloud!

—Henry Wadsworth Longfellow

PRAYER OF DEDICATION

MUSIC: "Serve the Lord With Gladness" (B. B. McKinney), or "Our Best" (S. C. Kirk, Grant Colfax Tullar), by youth choir and congregation.

BENEDICTION

DUE